I Thought I Was Changed

Walking in Transformation

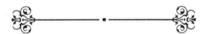

Book Three

Walking with Jesus

Becoming the Best Me I Can Be

Pamela D White

A publication of Blooming Desert Ministries

ISBN 978-1-7370802-4-4 (sc print)
ISBN 978-1-7370802-5-1 (ebook)

Printed in the United States of America
Copyright © 2021 by Pamela D White
All Rights Reserved.

IngramSparks Publishing (Ingram: Lightning Source, LLC)

One Ingram Blvd., La Vergne, TN 37086

Publishing Note: Publishing style capitalizes certain pronouns in Scriptures that refer to the Father, Son, and Holy Spirit, and may differ from other publishing styles. **All emphasis in the Scriptures' quotations is the authors.** The name satan and related names are not capitalized as the author's preference not to acknowledge him, even though it violates grammatical rules.

PDW PUBLICATIONS

Dedication

This book series is dedicated to you.

Everyone has opportunities to become a better version of themselves. My prayer is that this book series helps you on that journey. The Lord loves you so much He desires an intimate relationship with you. You are special to Him and He loves spending time with you. Walking and talking with Jesus every day should be the norm, not the exception. Life can bring difficult circumstances and situations. When you walk with Jesus, life events, are not only manageable but can be turned for your good.

"And we know that all things work together for good to those who love God, to those who are the called according to His purpose," Romans 8:28.

Come with me into this exploration of how you can develop a relationship with Jesus and walk with Him every day. This is an opportunity to become a better you.

Acknowledgments

The Great Commission given by our Lord and Savior Jesus Christ noted in Matthew 28:16-20 is my inspiration for this publication. Verses 19-20 state, *"Go therefore and make disciples of all the nations, baptizing them in the name of the Father and of the Son and of the Holy Spirit, teaching them to observe all things that I have commanded you; and lo, I am with you always, even to the end of the age."* This verse is the very basis for missionary work all over the globe. I have been blessed to be able to serve in a few of those missions. Missions are an amazing experience. I came to realize though that everyone cannot always do all the parts commanded in these verses. I can't always go. I didn't often get to baptize. What I realized was that I can do my part in teaching to observes the truths of the Scriptures. My desire to fulfill the teaching part of the Great Commission was the inspiration for this work. My pastor, Bishop Larry Taylor, and First Lady Desetra Taylor allowed our church to use these Bible studies in our New Life Discipleship classes for nearly twenty years. The work has also been used in prison ministries in central Illinois for as many years. The teaching has proven effective in changing many lives and discipling the children of God. Thank you, Bishop and First Lady, for teaching a balanced spiritual and natural life so I could complete this project and see the impact of the work on people's lives.

Bishop positioned me to be the director of New Life Ministries Discipleship for several years. New Life classes were designed to teach those new to Christianity or new to the church the foundational truths needed to build a solid life in Christ. During that time, this work was fine-tuned with the help and input from the dedicated, gifted, and anointed New Life teachers Minister Retta Smith, Minister James Smith, Minister Debby Henkel, Dr. Terry Husband, Minister Char-Michelle McDowell, Minister Yvonne Smith, Minister Herbert Smyer, and Professor Susan Gibson along with the encouragement and guidance of Dr. Chequita Brown and community service advocate Minister Patricia Turner. I also want to give a shout-out to Dr. Wanda Turner, nationally acclaimed minister, teacher, prophet, life coach, mentor, and best-selling author, who continued to encourage me to just publish the thing! Thanks to all of you. Each of you has made a significant impact on my life.

My dear friend and mentor, First Lady Marshell Wickware, supported the project and pushed me to publish it for years. Thanks for not giving up on me!

My life-long friend, Robin McClallen, thank you for all your support, input, and encouraging me to publish something. You have been instrumental in making me an author.

A special thanks to my husband, Brian K. White, for his patience and prayers as I spent hours and hours researching, writing, and rewriting. Thanks, BW!

Most of all thank you to the Holy Spirit and my Lord and Savior Jesus Christ. I present this work in obedience and honor to You.

Contents

Book Three

I Thought I Was Changed
Walking in Transformation

OBJECTIVE

As a Christian, you are a disciple or follower of Christ. In following Christ, you are to put off the old sin nature and transform your body, soul, and spirit to be more like Christ. With this in mind, there are tools to equip you so you can grow in Christ. It will challenge you to model godly behavior as exemplified in the biblical text. Spiritual growth is not a passive activity; you must make an active decision to grow in God. Transformation is not automatic. It requires your obedience and committed heart. Then you will see outward evidence of your inward commitment to Christ.

MEMORY VERSES

"I am the vine, you are the branches: He that stays in me, and I in him, the same brings forth much fruit: for without me you can do nothing," John 15:5 AKJV.

"Therefore if any man be in Christ, he is a new creature: old things are passed away; behold, all things are become new," 2 Corinthians 5:17 KJV.

I Thought I Was Changed

A. Breaking the Bondage of the Past

    1. What is Deliverance?

    2. Power of Salvation

    3. You are a Three-Part Being

    4. Your Second Chance

    5. Transformation

B. Making a Choice to Grow and Mature

C. How to Free the Body and Soul

    1. Love the Lord with All Your Heart

    2. Desire to be Free of Sin and Bondage

    3. Practice Self-discipline

    4. Feed Your Spirit

    5. Read and Meditate on the Word

    6. Make Godly Choices

    7. Fellowship With Believers

    8. Apply God's Word

    9. Listen to the Holy Spirit

    10. Resist Sin

    11. Develop Spiritual Gifts

    12. Become a Fruit Bearer

D. Results of Transformation

E. Benefits of Growing in Christ

Book Three

I Thought I Was Changed
Walking in Transformation
Introduction

Salvation renews fellowship with the Father. To maintain this relationship unhindered by sin, you must grow and mature. We call this transformation. It is a complete makeover. Sin puts you in chains and bondage. Salvation sets you free to develop and mature, becoming more like Christ. Transformation requires daily decisions that support godliness and holiness. Accepting Christ was only the initial step; now it's time to continue your transformation by fully connecting to God through Bible study, prayer, and fellowship with other Christians. As you maintain these connections, the Word of God will bring deliverance to your body, soul, and spirit.

Breaking the Bondage
of the Past

—◆—

WHAT IS DELIVERANCE?

Deliverance means to be rescued or set free. What do you need to be rescued from? Here are just a few strongholds to start you thinking about what might keep you bound: depression, oppression, fear, rejection, anger, abandonment, lying, lack, shame, addictions, grief, lust, despair, pride, mental illness, laziness, curses and so much more. Hopefully, that short list sheds light on some areas in your life that need transformation. Though you become a new creation when you accept Christ, there is a process of being separated from your old nature and habits. We call the process deliverance. The definition of deliverance is the act of being set free or rescued from any form of restraint whether mentally, physically, emotionally, or spiritually. We all need deliverance from something, so don't feel you are the only one. That is a common tactic of the enemy, to make you feel you are alone in your battle. You are not alone and you are not the only person struggling with whatever bondage the Holy Spirit reveals to you. That's kind of key. Holy Spirit has to reveal it. You can try to figure out what deliverance you need and just might have some success, but when the Holy Spirit reveals the real root of your bondage, deliverance is imminent. God's will is for you to be free. If you ask Him, He will show you what you need to know. Just ask. Let's talk about what that looks like.

POWER OF SALVATION

Through salvation, Jesus rescued you and gave you the **POWER TO BREAK THE CHAINS** of sin and bondage in your life. Walking away from old habits, mindsets, and behaviors is not always easy. Sometimes bondage results from your choices. Sometimes, generations from your parents, grandparents, great grandparents, or even farther back in your genealogy pass down bondages. 'You're just like your father!' 'Stop acting like Aunt Sue!' The stronger your relationship with Christ and the more you endeavor to apply God's Word to your life, the easier it will be for you to cultivate godly character, living in freedom and liberty.

You are a Three-part Being

Remember from book one *There Must be a Better Way* in the *Walking with Jesus* series, you are a three-part being. You are a composition of body, soul, and spirit. You are a spiritual being that has a soul and lives in a body. Your body is the physical you. It experiences pain, pleasure, and other sensations experienced through your five senses. Your soul includes your mind, will, and emotions. Before salvation, your thoughts are largely generated from your soul. You experienced your emotions through your soul. You made decisions through your soul experiences. Your spirit is the piece of you that longs for a connection with a Higher Being. It is the part of God that He left in you when He created you. Until you connect to God through salvation, it lies dormant with a beacon of longing desiring to reconnect with the Creator.

Your transformation begins with salvation and makes it possible for deliverance, freeing your soul and body from bondage. Until the point of salvation, your soul and body have been running the show. Your body has requirements or demands such as sleep, hunger, thirst, and many more. Your unrenewed body wants those demands met as quickly and effectively as possible. The soul runs by a series of emotions that mostly want to bring you whatever you want and need. This is humanity at its most selfish. Your body and soul have suffered wounds, sickness, and many other things. As you embrace your transformation and allow deliverance, your renewed spirit grows. Your body and spirit experience healing. As your spirit grows and matures, it becomes your 'go to' rather than the selfish needs of your body or soul. Your body learns to be quiet and obey the spirit. Your mind and emotions learn to put away ungodly thoughts and stop giving in to every whim of your emotions. You grow away from selfishness and develop into a servant of God. As you mature, your body, soul, and spirit come into sync and work together.

When you accept Christ into your life, your spirit is reborn. Many people think this means that everything is automatically great now. They have the misconception that bad things can't happen anymore. They may think that this new beginning takes away the past. You have a fresh start in life, a second chance, and an opportunity to change. You are a new creation, reconnected to your Creator, who generates new life. Yet, your body and soul haven't changed—yet. Your life circumstances are still the same— for now. You still think the same. You still look the same. However, the Father is not 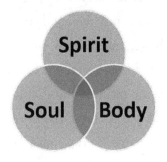 just concerned with renewing your spirit. He wants you to live a balanced, healthy life for all three of your parts. He wants your body healthy and your mind healed and whole just like your spirit has become. Each time you make a choice for Christ, the strength of your spirit grows. Every area of your life represents this transformation. The new spirit in you empowers you to bring change to your soul and body through Christ. Your old thought patterns rarely line up with God's perfect will for you. They act as chains and bondages that hold you to your old way of living and thinking, keeping you from the **PERFECT DESTINY** that God has prepared for you.

"The righteous shall flourish like the palm tree: he shall grow like a cedar in Lebanon," Psalm 92:12.

Your Second Chance

The body and soul have been trapped in bondage to sin since birth. Because of the disobedience of Adam in the Garden of Eden, your body and soul are born in sin and trapped. No matter how hard you try, you still sin. That lie fell out of your mouth. You said or did something hurtful, stole what you knew you shouldn't have, and chose you over someone else. Sometime in your life, you sinned. So now what? When the spirit is reborn, it is your opportunity to become free from sin forever. That doesn't mean that you won't make mistakes or make a wrong choice. It means you have a chance to live a different kind of life. It also means you have a chance to experience forgiveness and start over. You have a second chance.

Transformation

Transformation is a complete change, a different configuration. It isn't just putting a hat and mustache on an old idea. It is a complete and thorough conversion. As a follower of Christ and a child of God, you transform your thought patterns from the old carnal state of mind to the mind of Christ. Carnal means you understand how you should live and act, but act according to your selfish desires even though it's against the will of God. We call this living according to the flesh or the needs of your body and soul. Romans 8 has a lot to say about that. I encourage you to read the whole chapter. Here is a brief excerpt regarding carnality vs. living according to the Spirit.

"There is therefore now no condemnation to those who are in Christ Jesus, who do not walk according to the flesh, but according to the Spirit. For the law of the Spirit of life in Christ Jesus has made me free from the law of sin and death. For what the law could not do in that it was weak through the flesh, God did by sending His own Son in the likeness of sinful flesh, on account of sin: He condemned sin in the flesh, that the righteous requirement of the law might be fulfilled in us who do not walk according to the flesh but according to the Spirit. For those who live according to the flesh set their minds on the things of the flesh, but those who live according to the Spirit, the

things of the Spirit. For to be carnally minded is death, but to be spiritually minded is life and peace. Because the carnal mind is enmity against God; for it is not subject to the law of God, nor indeed can be. So then, those who are in the flesh cannot please God. But you are not in the flesh but in the Spirit, if indeed the Spirit of God dwells in you. Now if anyone does not have the Spirit of Christ, he is not His. And if Christ is in you, the body is dead because of sin, but the Spirit is life because of righteousness. But if the Spirit of Him who raised Jesus from the dead dwells in you, He who raised Christ from the dead will also give life to your mortal bodies through His Spirit who dwells in you," Romans 8: 1-11.

Carnality differs from someone spiritually immature or new to Christianity. Like newborn babies, a new Christian has not had the time to mature. They are still in training. Carnal Christians are people who received teaching but choose not to live what they have been taught. It is difficult for a carnal-minded person to grow spiritually in Christ. It's your choice. You can choose to transform or you can choose to live the same as you did before. Romans 8 says to live carnally minded is to choose death, so it's not a wise choice. A Christian should look different from those who are not yet Christians. To remain the same as everyone is an unfulfilled life and a dead life. A carnal life has no peace because it's a life of selfishness.

"Do not conform to the pattern of this world, but be transformed by the renewing of your mind. Then you will be able to test and approve what God's will is--his good, pleasing and perfect will," Romans 12:2 NIV.

The life of a caterpillar is the perfect example of what your transformation will look like. A caterpillar is born to the earth, crawling around living a life bound to survival. Then it begins its transformation by building a cocoon or chrysalis. Transformation begins with the caterpillar melting down. It becomes a puddle of goo, all except for the heart. Metamorphosis creates a new being out of the goo around the heart. That new being that emerges is an amazingly beautiful butterfly. You too can give up your life of crawling around bound to the earth just trying to get your needs met and experience a drastic transformation or metamorphosis and become a free-flying beautiful creation.

Making a Choice to Grow and Mature

God desires for you to grow in your relationship with Him. However, you must choose to commit to the process. Remember, growth in God is not passive; it is a daily, active engagement in your growth process. You cannot idly sit by and expect change in your life without putting forth effort. The choice is yours - to grow or not to grow. If you decide to grow in God, know that there will be opposition.

You have two enemies. Your first and most dangerous enemy is YOU! You truly are your own worst enemy. Your fleshly desire, old mindsets, lusts, pride, selfishness, and disobedience want only your destruction. You can destroy yourself faster than anyone else. The worst part is you can't even get away from yourself. Everywhere you go; there you are with all your selfishness and self-destruction. What does fighting against you look like? You choose selfishly instead of according to the will of God, think negatively, dwell on the past, and rehearse hurts and pain instead of choosing forgiveness. You self-criticize, make excuses, and devalue yourself. You don't set boundaries or adhere to the boundaries of others. You get stuck in mindlessness—stuck in a rut. You surround yourself with negative people instead of building a supporting tribe and blame God or others for your own choices and the negative results of those choices. That is why the Apostle Paul is so adamant in Romans 12:2, telling you to not conform to the pattern of the world. By 'the world' we mean those who don't know Jesus and don't live righteously. Paul is saying not to be like those who live selfishly and unrighteous, but to choose change.

Your other enemy is satan who is the enemy of God and His children. Satan was once an angel of heaven. He was a worshiping angel named Lucifer who had the idea that he could run things better than God. Lucifer thought he should be honored more than God. He had self-centered ideas of grandeur. As a result, he was thrown out of heaven. He took one-third of the angelic force with him causing a major heavenly war. You can read more about Lucifer's fall in Ezekiel 28 and Isaiah 14. He hates the children of God and will do everything he can to kill, steal and/or destroy God's people, including you. Satan is no match against the power of God, but he puts up a good fight by attacking God's children. He does this in a variety of ways. Satan whispers thoughts to you and tries to make you think those thoughts are your own. He will try to trap you and trick you. Satan loves deception, distraction, and lies. He is known in scripture as the father of lies. He will attack your body and try many things to stop you from serving God. He doesn't want you to understand the power of God because then you can trounce him. The enemy of your soul works through media, TV, movies, governments, friends, loved ones, and enemies. (For more on how to win the battle against this enemy, see "Walking Strong.")

Here are a few of the enemy's tactics. There are many, many more. This is just a small taste of the bitter pill he sticks in the peanut butter of life.

Depression	Anxiety	Low Self-esteem	Lies & half-truths
Fear	Worry	Selfishness	Witchcraft
Jealousy	Disobedience	Hatred	Disease
Doubt	Religion	Adultery	Addictions
Pride	Distrust	Unbelief	Lack of Self-control
Deception	Discouragement	Diversion	Confusion
Defeat	Delay	Division	Temptations
Intimidation	Theft	Exhaustion	Exploit Weaknesses
Mental Illness	Rejection	Lack	Strife

How to Free the Body and Soul

With your mind and an unseen enemy so diligently working against you, a peaceful life may seem impossible. The transformation we have been discussing is the process to go through to overcome both sin-nature and satan. Overcoming sin nature occurs through a process called sanctification. Part of that process is deliverance. You must want deliverance. God's will is that you are free from everything that holds you back from your destiny. You also have a will. A will is a choice, an inclination, or a determination. Your will is your ability to choose. Your will must meet God's will. God's will is that you are free from the bondages of sin. When your will is to be free and you desire is to walk in obedience to God, then deliverance is not only possible, it is imminent.

Your body has had a lot to say about the choices you've made up to the point of your decision to accept Jesus as Savior. It demanded food when it was hungry and let you know when it was thirsty and required water. The skin itched when it needed a shower. Nerves felt pain when you got too close to a fire. When you felt alone or scared or just plain hungry, your body craved pizza and chocolate. Your body lied and told you it wouldn't survive if it didn't get what it wanted. It has been demanding things from you for your entire life. As the spirit-man in you grows, you will put your body into subjection to your spirit. The body will not give up control easily. The body is only your temporary home and will perish. **YOUR SPIRIT LIVES FOREVER.** The body wants selfishly. It must learn to be in subjection to the Spirit. The body had a significant amount of control and it did everything it can to silence your spirit. The influence of the body's desires will do everything possible to keep the spirit-man small and immature. This is a major battle for many believers.

Another major battle is the war that rages in your mind. Your thoughts are powerful. Thoughts become words. Words become actions. Actions become habits. Habits become character. Character becomes your eternity. Your choices of the thoughts you entertain ultimately make you who you are. When you entertain negative thoughts, the result is sin, hate, depression, destruction—all the negative stuff. When you entertain positive thoughts or God-like thoughts, the result is peace and blessing—all the positive stuff. All kinds of thoughts can run through your head. That doesn't mean you thought those thoughts. There are influences all around you. Your job is to filter. It is only those thoughts you choose to dwell on that have the potential to alter your life.

"Finally, brothers and sisters, whatever is true, whatever is noble, whatever is right, whatever is pure, whatever is lovely, whatever is admirable—if anything is excellent or praiseworthy—think about such things," Philippians 5:8 NIV.

There are some things you can do to **WIN THE BATTLE** against your thoughts, fleshly disobedience, carnality, or the insistent demands of your body.

Here are a few.

1. Love the Lord
2. Desire to be free
3. Self-Discipline
4. Feed your spirit
5. Read and meditate on the Word
6. Make godly choices
7. Fellowship with believers
8. Apply God's Word
9. Listen to the Holy Spirit
10. Resist sin
11. Develop spiritual gifts
12. Become a fruit bearer

LOVE THE LORD

Loving the Lord is like any relationship. It takes time. Relationship building is a process. When you develop a love for the Lord, it produces obedience and service to the Lord. You walk in obedience to God and His Word (the Bible). That means if God says don't steal, then you don't steal. When the Bible says don't lie, then you don't lie. Just like when mom said no cookies before dinner, you didn't eat the cookies. OK, so you took the cookies, and sometimes you might find that you didn't obey God's commands. If you find yourself in that predicament, then ask for forgiveness. He is faithful to forgive when you truthfully repent or turn from doing something that is against His commands. Obeying His commands shows you not only love Him, but you trust Him. You serve God faithfully. There are fewer and fewer times when you choose what you want over what God desires for you or over what God has commanded in His Word. Serving Him shows you love Him.

"If you love me, keep my commandments," John 14:15 AKJV.

"But without faith it is impossible to please him: for he that cometh to God must believe that he is, and that he is a rewarder of them that diligently seek him," Hebrews 11:6 KJV.

DESIRE TO BE FREE OF SIN AND BONDAGE

You must desire to be free. If you don't want it, then you don't get it. To some of you that might seem weird. Why wouldn't someone want to be free? Surprisingly, there are some people more comfortable in their pain and shackles.

BEING FREE CAN FEEL INTIMIDATING when you are used to bondage. You've probably heard stories of released prisoners who commit crimes just so they are re-incarcerated where life is familiar. They may have hated prison, but freedom is more frightening because it's unfamiliar and over-whelming territory. For some people that is true of spiritual freedom as well. God created you to be free and He desires that you live in freedom and not be burdened with bondages. Hang in there and you can learn to live free.

"Stand fast therefore in the liberty wherewith Christ hath made us free, and be not entangled again with the yoke of bondage," Galatians 5:1 KJV.

"You, my brothers and sisters, were called to be free," Galatians 5:13 NIV.

Practice Self-Discipline

To make the voice of your body quieter and put it in subjection to your spirit, you must discipline the body. It won't like it and will do what it can to rebel against you. When you say no, it tries to trick you into just one more piece of cake or just a little more sleep. You probably taught your body to get up at a certain time of day so you can do what you have to do like work or school. If you can do that when you weren't a Christian, then you can certainly train your body with the power of Christ on your side. Some things you can do to discipline your body and mind are fasting and prayer.

Fasting. Fasting is a spiritual tool that puts your body and mind in subjection or submission to your spirit. Fasting is a time when you abstain from food while you focus on prayer. The purpose is not to lose weight, but to provide unique spiritual insights. Fasting requires self-control and discipline. It puts the things of this physical world second to the things of the spiritual world, thus bringing you closer to God. It helps you hear God more clearly while quieting the demands of your body. Fasting also helps you focus your mind. It is a time to focus on the Lord and His will rather than video games, movies, or TV. It can be tough, but worth it. There are several ways to fast. The important thing is that you put your body in subjection and seek the Lord during that time. (**For medical reasons, some people may not be able to fast from food altogether. A better choice may be to choose to abstain from certain foods like sweets or something other than food like social media or entertainment like television. Never stop taking medications without consulting your physician.)

PRAYER. Prayer is another spiritual tool that also puts your mind and body in subjection to the spirit. It may not seem like prayer has anything to do with your body, but just try to pray for ten minutes. Your body will try to go to sleep, look out the window, crave a snack, listen to the neighbors, or any of a zillion other things just so you pay attention to it rather than pray. Prayer takes discipline and self-control to concentrate on your conversation with God rather than what is going on around you. Prayer and fasting are necessary for some levels of deliverance, as noted in the book of Matthew. For more on prayer, please see "Time in the Garden".

"However, this kind goes not out but by prayer and fasting," Matthew 17:21 AKJV.

FEED YOUR SPIRIT

Your body needs food and water or it dies. The mind needs inspiration, or it becomes dormant. Your spirit also needs to be fed. You must be careful what you put in your spirit. What goes in is what comes out. If you feed your body donuts and pizza day after day, then your health will decline rapidly. You suffer from malnutrition and your internal organs get sick. If you feed your spirit with soap operas, murderous video games, filthy language, etc. then don't be surprised at the decline of your spirit. Just like your body needs nutritious food and fresh water to flourish, it is important to feed your spirit with the best nutrients. The influence of the world is all around you. It is your choice what to feed your spirit. Be selective in your TV shows, video games, movies, music, and reading material. If Jesus and your momma wouldn't approve, then stop it. Find things that do not disrespect God to put into your spirit. Things that help you build faith and give honor to the Lord.

"As newborn babes, desire the sincere milk of the word, that ye may grow thereby: If so be ye have tasted that the Lord is gracious," 1 Peter 2:2-3 KJV.

"Blessed are they which do hunger and thirst after righteousness: for they shall be filled," Matthew 5:6 KJV.

READ AND MEDITATE ON THE WORD OF GOD

The Word of God is the Holy Bible. It is an inspirational love letter from the Lord to you that has everything you need for every situation. The Word is your strength. It is **LIFEBLOOD RUNNING THROUGH YOUR SPIRITUAL VEINS**. Without the Word, you become emaciated and weak. With the Word, you become prosperous in every area of your life in ways you could never imagine. Reading the Bible is how you get to know God, learn His ways and find your destiny and purpose. You can't just read it though. Reading the Bible is just a start. It isn't a Facebook story you see today and forget tomorrow. To gain strength and insight from the Word, you need to take time to meditate and ask the Lord what it means. Meditating on the truths found in God's Word differs from meditation practices associated with some Eastern religions. Meditation practices are about training the mind and using mantras to take you to a realm that can be full of deception. Meditating on the Word is about taking the Word of God and hiding it in your heart and allowing the Lord to show you truths in Scripture and how to apply those truths to your life. When life throws things your way, the answer will be ready and waiting in that hidden place in your heart, and you will know how to meet the challenge with the power and insight of the Word.

"But his delight is in the law of the Lord, and in His law he meditates day and night," Psalm 1:2.

"This Book of the Law shall not depart from your mouth, but you shall meditate in it day and night, that you may observe to do according to all that is written in it. For then you will make your way prosperous, and then you will have good success," Joshua 1:8.

MAKE GODLY CHOICES

Every day, you can make godly choices in music, movies, TV, books, friends, time, finances, conversations, thought patterns and so much more. You have many opportunities each day to honor God faithfully in every choice you make. It's easy to make a selfish choice. You don't even have to think about that. It comes naturally to appease your selfish body and soulish emotions. Godly choices take discipline and awareness. As you practice making godly choices, those choices become the norm while selfish choices fall away.

"If any of you lack wisdom, let him ask of God, that giveth to all men liberally, and upbraideth not; and it shall be given him," James 1:5 KJV.

FELLOWSHIP WITH BELIEVERS

God adopts you into His family to help you through hard times and to help you rejoice in victorious times. We need each other. We keep each other accountable, which helps each other grow and flourish and pick each other up when we fall. Fellowshipping isn't just about attending church. Life is too short for just being a Sunday morning saint. It's about spending time with other believers, have lunch, go to a movie, take a trip, go on the mission field, volunteer, help a neighbor and enjoy the gift of life.

"And let us consider one another in order to stir up love and good works, not forsaking the assembling of ourselves together, as is the manner of some, but exhorting one another, and so much the more as you see the Day approaching," Hebrews 10:24-25.

Apply God's Word

God's Word is to be applied to life situations. It is the power that turns impossible circumstances into possible solutions. The Bible is not just an old storybook or a historical account. God's Word is filled with life and love. The Scriptures provide the answers to all of life's questions. There are no impossible situations. God has the answers to everything. When you read, memorize, and meditate on the Word, it becomes a part of you. As you make life's decisions, the Word in you will guide, encourage, provide, and sustain you through life's decisions, transforming you from your old self to be more like Christ.

"Therefore lay aside all filthiness and overflow of wickedness, and receive with meekness the implanted word, which is able to save your souls. But be doers of the word, and not hearers only, deceiving yourselves. For if anyone is a hearer of the word and not a doer, he is like a man observing his natural face in a mirror; for he observes himself, goes away, and immediately forgets what kind of man he was," James 1:21-23.

Learn to Listen to the Holy Spirit

The Holy Spirit will provide wisdom, understanding, and encouragement to you. He will teach you about God and His ways. He will help you serve others and love others unconditionally. Every day there are decisions before you. Some doors open and others close and you have to choose all over again. Decisions can be as simple as what to wear today or as complicated as life-impacting medical decisions. All you have to do is be still, listen, tune into the flow of the Holy Spirit. Then be obedient to what you hear from the Spirit of God. When you train yourself to hear what the Spirit is saying to you, your whole life will change. Remember, the Holy Spirit will never speak against the Word of God or against God's will. If what you hear doesn't line up with the Word, then it wasn't God speaking.

"And he said unto them, Take heed what ye hear: with what measure ye mete, it shall be measured to you: and unto you that hear shall more be given," Mark 4:24 KJV.

"Behold, I stand at the door, and knock: if any man hear my voice, and open the door, I will come in to him, and will sup with him, and he with me," Revelation 3:20 KJV.

RESIST SIN

Before the Lord was in your life, it was easy to make selfish choices. When you accepted Jesus into your life, your transformation began. The world around you didn't transform with you. The same temptations, deceptions, and traps still seek you out. As a Spirit-filled Christian, the Spirit empowered you to resist the old temptations. When those old things attempt to distract you from God's way, you can now say no. No doubt about it, resisting sin can be a fierce struggle. God is faithful. He hasn't left you unequipped or alone. Keep on resisting and making wise choices.

"No temptation has overtaken you except what is common to humankind. And God is faithful; he will not let you be tempted beyond what you can bear. But when you are tempted, he will also provide a way out so that you can endure it," 1 Corinthians 10:13.

Develop Spiritual Gifts

The Lord gives every person gifts. You may have one gift or find that you have multiple gifts. You can put your gifts on a shelf in the closet for later use, bury them in the backyard so you can forget them, or develop them and use them. I'd like to see you put that awesome-looking Christmas or birthday gift on a back shelf without exploring it! The Lord gives gifts to you so you can help others and do good deeds. I encourage you not to shelve them or hide them and to do whatever you can to develop your gifts. Take a class, read a book, or volunteer. Just do something to increase the growth of your gifts.

"For to one is given the word of wisdom through the Spirit, to another the word of knowledge through the same Spirit, to another faith by the same Spirit, to another gifts of healings by the same Spirit, to another the working of miracles, to another prophecy, to another discerning of spirits, to another different kinds of tongues, to another the interpretation of tongues," 1 Corinthians 12:8-10.

Become a Fruit Bearer

You are a garden in a thankless dark desert of a world. You are the source of sustenance to a dying people. Too corny? Maybe. But it's true.

You have spiritual fruit with the ability to feed the world. The Lord wants you to grow spiritual fruit and then give away your spiritual fruit to help others. Spiritual fruit shows the character of God through you. The fruit of the spirit is the manifestation of God's love through you by the power of the Holy Spirit. It is the outward evidence of your inward relationship with Christ. Though there are nine attributes listed, the word *fruit* is singular, meaning they work as one. You cannot pick which fruit to grow; it's all or nothing!

"But the fruit of the Spirit is love, joy, peace, longsuffering, gentleness, goodness, faith, meekness, temperance: against such there is no law," Galatians 5:22-23 KJV.

Results of Transformation

Spiritual growth is not a passive activity; you must daily choose to seek God for spiritual growth and actively engage in the transformation process. Change is difficult, but **IT'S WORTH IT!** When you commit yourself to walk in God's ways no matter what and keep talking to the Lord about everything, your transformation will continue.

"Commit your way to the Lord, trust also in Him, and He shall bring it to pass," Psalm 37:5 KJV.

"Be anxious for nothing, but in everything by prayer and supplication, with thanksgiving, let your requests be made known to God; and the peace of God, which surpasses all understanding, will guard your hearts and minds through Christ Jesus," Philippians 4:6-7.

As you strengthen your relationship with God through prayer and meditating on God's Word, changes occur in your life. You get results. Circumstances change. Your attitude toward life changes. Here are some of those changes you and others will see.

1. Your connection to and desire for sinful habits and behaviors weaken as your transformation progresses. I had a friend who was a chain smoker. He had smoked since he was a teenager. When he

decided to lead a life of Christianity and discipleship, he decided he wanted to stop smoking. He tried all the 'normal' solutions. He did nicotine patches, nicotine gum, candy, exercise, and other remedies that didn't work. Sometimes he could stop for a few days and didn't smoke at all. Some days he couldn't put the cigarettes down. He gave up a few times for a minute or two. There were days when it seemed like it would never happen. He kept reading the scriptures. He kept praying and asking God for help. Then one day he realized he liked the cravings. He liked the nicotine, and he liked how the cigarettes made him feel. When he realized that quitting smoking was just an idea and not a desire, he changed his attitude and approach toward his goal. He thought that if he just told God he wanted to stop smoking, God would miraculously deliver him even though he kept buying smokes. That day he realized the problem was his, not God's. He threw out the pack he kept at work. His will to stop smoking met God's will for him to take care of his body. Soon when he got out of bed, he realized he didn't crave a smoke. It was almost time for him to go home from work before he realized he hadn't smoked all day. Every day was a victory and another step farther from the bondage he had felt to the addiction. It has been over thirty years since he decided to do his part, change his attitude, and believe that when his will met God's will then he would be free. Whatever you need deliverance from, the same freedom can be yours.

"But I say, walk and live [habitually] in the [Holy] Spirit [responsive to and controlled and guided by the Spirit]; then you will certainly not gratify the cravings and desires of the flesh (of human nature without God). For the desires of the flesh are opposed to the [Holy]

Spirit, and the [desires of the] Spirit are opposed to the flesh (godless human nature); for these are antagonistic to each other [continually withstanding and in conflict with each other], so that you are not free but are prevented from doing what you desire to do. But if you are guided (led) by the [Holy] Spirit, you are not subject to the Law," Galatians 5:16-18 AMP.

2. Christ-like characteristics develop. That doesn't mean you aren't you anymore. Your personality is still very much intact. After all, God created your personality just for you. You will develop character traits that represent Christ. Following are some of those character traits:

Faithfulness	Commitment	Flexibility	Forgiveness
Focus	Patience	Being Teachable	Humility
Courage	Fairness	Honesty	Friendships
Dependability	Responsibility	Generosity	Contentment
Gratitude	Loyalty	Hospitality	Encouragement
Confidence	Wisdom	Diligence	Compassion
Discretion	Obedience	Conviction	Creativity
Endurance	Grace	Integrity	Patience
Purpose	Tolerance	Understanding	Strength

"For I have given you an example, that ye should do as I have done to you," John 13:15 KJV.

"For whom he did foreknow, he also did predestinate to be conformed to the image of his Son, that he might be the firstborn among many brethren," Romans 8:29 KJV.

41

3. You develop a greater understanding of your new identity in Christ. Up to this point, you have had an identity that your past has created. Chances are that there are chunks of that identity that aren't true or accurate. As a new creation in Christ, you became a new creation and received adoption into the family of Christ. It takes time to understand who you are in this combo of your past, present, and brand-new future. I encourage you to keep exploring who God created you to be.

"Therefore if any man be in Christ, he is a new creature: old things are passed away; behold, all things are become new," 2 Corinthians 5:17 KJV.

"But we all, with open face beholding as in a glass the glory of the Lord, are changed into the same image from glory to glory, even as by the Spirit of the Lord," 2 Corinthians 3:18 KJV.

"But ye are a chosen generation, a royal priesthood, an holy nation, a peculiar people; that ye should shew forth the praises of him who hath called you out of darkness into his marvellous light: Which in time past were not a people, but are now the people of God: which had not obtained mercy, but now have obtained mercy," 1 Peter 2:9-10 KJV.

4. You grow in spiritual awareness of your role in the kingdom of God and your purpose for life increases. As a child of God, you have a **KINGDOM PURPOSE**. You also have a role in the family of God. The more you read the word and pray, the more you become aware of and fulfill the role created for you and the purpose you were destined to complete.

"Thou wilt keep him in perfect peace, whose mind is stayed on thee: because he trusteth in thee. Trust ye in the Lord for ever: for in the Lord Jehovah is everlasting strength," Isaiah 26:3-4 KJV.

"Our purpose is to do what is right, not only in the sight of the Lord, but also in the sight of others," 2 Corinthians 8:21 GNT.

5. You become more accustomed to submitting your life to Christ as a living sacrifice and thus transform into the likeness of Christ. In your old sin nature, your choices were probably mostly selfish or self-seeking. As you submit yourself to God's word and make godly choices, your life becomes a living sacrifice. What does it mean to be a living sacrifice? Well, it doesn't mean that you punish yourself or offer yourself as a sacrifice like the Old Testament animal sacrifices. It means that although you are in a world of selfishness, lust, and pride that you choose against what your selfish desires want and choose unselfishly. Transformation means you work on changing your thought patterns so lust doesn't rule your actions. It means you understand **GOD IS GOD AND YOU ARE NOT** God, therefore; you need Him to guide you through your life. Christ is the only one that needed to die on a cross. Submitting to Christ means you accept His sacrifice on the cross and choose to die to your selfish desires so that you may live the life prepared for you.

"Therefore, I urge you, brothers and sisters, in view of God's mercy, to offer your bodies as a living sacrifice, holy and pleasing to God--this is your true and proper worship. Do not conform to the pattern of this world, but be transformed by the renewing of your mind. Then you will be able to test and approve what God's will is--his good, pleasing and perfect will," Romans 12:1-2 NIV.

6. You grow in your knowledge and understanding of the nature and character of Christ. To be like Christ, you kind of need to know what He's like. What better way to know who He is, what He would do in a situation, how He interacts with people, and all the things that make Him, Jesus, than to read about Him in God's word, talk to Him and get to know Him, adjust your thinking to be like His, and imitate His perfect example.

"For whom he did foreknow, he also did predestinate to be conformed to the image of his Son, that he might be the firstborn among many brethren," Romans 8:29 KJV.

The Benefits of Growing in Christ

Cultivating a strong and growing relationship with Christ requires an active effort on your part. If you want to be a brilliant pianist, you can't just sit around and never touch the piano keys. Maybe you want to be a skilled basketball player. Well, you have to spend practice time practicing with a basketball. If you want to fulfill a great destiny, do your part. The result of your commitment to growing in God has eternal rewards.

- You experience the sovereignty of God. He is the ruler of the universe. He owns everything and has complete control over everything. Now don't get it twisted. That doesn't mean God controls you. You have free will and can make choices. It isn't God that makes bad things happen. **YOU ARE NOT A VICTIM** of a heartless sovereign deity. God wants you to have peace, rest, prosperity, and authority. God told Adam and Eve to take pleasure in His creation and have dominion over it, being fruitful, and multiplying. Your peace, rest, prosperity, and authority were surrendered and put under subjection to Satan when the first man, Adam, disobeyed God's instructions. Authority on earth switched into the hands of Satan. That's why bad things happen, because of Satan's earthly authority and man's sin-nature. Through God's covenant and Jesus' blood sacrifice, the surrendered authority was returned to earth. As a child of God, you now have the authority to take back everything stolen. You can have peace, rest, and prosperity with your restored authority. In the blink of an eye, God could start over with a different universe, new worlds, and new people. But He has chosen you to rule and reign in your world.

"Yours, O Lord, is the greatness, the power and the glory, the victory and the majesty; for all that is in heaven and in earth is Yours; Yours is the kingdom, O Lord, and You are exalted as head over all. Both riches and honor come from You, and You reign over all. In Your hand is power and might; in Your hand it is to make great and to give strength to all" 1 Chronicles 29:11-12.

- You learn to distinguish your ways from God's ways. You feel like punching the jerk who just cut you off in traffic. God has another idea. There is a temptation to grab a piece of fruit from the produce bin at the grocery store because you are hungry and it's just sitting there, but God calls that stealing. You want to watch that sexy movie, but God says you can't handle it and need to choose something else. Then, you try to tell your neighbor "God said... whatever" when you know it was your excuse for something you just want to happen, want to do, or don't want to do. God thinks on a different level than you or I. You want what you want, but it may not be good for you in the big picture. God can see your life from the beginning of time to the very end, so He might just have a better perspective on what is best. As you get to know God and

His ways, you will differentiate what thoughts and ideas are yours and what came from the throne of God.

"For the word of God is quick, and powerful, and sharper than any two-edged sword, piercing even to the dividing asunder of soul and spirit, and of the joints and marrow, and is a discerner of the thoughts and intents of the heart," Hebrews 4:12 KJV.

"For My thoughts are not your thoughts, nor are your ways My ways," says the Lord. *"For as the heavens are higher than the earth, so are My ways higher than your ways, and My thoughts than your thoughts"* Isaiah 55:8-9.

- You exercise patience and learn to be still in God's presence. It's hard to wait. You might know what your purpose and destiny are and you have tried every which way to get there when all you might need to do is be still and wait for God to make a way for you. You might see a promise in the Word and start trying with all your might to achieve victory with that scripture. The Lord wants you to pursue your destiny and believe the scriptures work for you. Often God's children try so hard to make things happen that nothing happens because they are doing things their way and not His. He says, 'Be still.' That doesn't mean you sit down and do nothing. Being still means relax. Stop stressing. Continue preparing, working, and believing. Don't be idle. Don't let go. Keep seeking God's will. Keep on keeping on, but don't stress. Trust that God works even when you can't see it and you are struggling to believe what the Word says for your life will happen.

"Be still, and know that I am God: I will be exalted among the heathen, I will be exalted in the earth" Psalm 46:10 AKJV.

- You identify yourself as victorious. The Word of God declares you are victorious. You know that is not how you feel all the time. Maybe you have never felt that way, ever. Being an overcomer and walking in victory may seem like very foreign things to experience. The more you communicate with the Lord through reading the Word, prayer, and fellowshipping with other believers, the closer you come to victory. Each victory you achieve is a stepping-stone to a greater victory. **KEEP ON FIGHTING**, pushing, and persevering. God has great things in store for you if you just don't give up.

"Blessed is the man who perseveres under trial, because when he has stood the test, he will receive the crown of life that God has promised to those who love him," James 1:12 NIV.

- You grow in fruitfulness, assurance, perseverance, and eternal blessing. We have already discussed these different areas. The important thing to remember is that you grow! You don't stay the same. Have you ever heard a new mom say she just wished her baby could stay little forever? That might seem like a lovely sentiment, but you know it's not realistic. If the child never grew or developed, the medical profession would confirm there was something seriously wrong and some disease or illness was probably preventing growth. If you do not grow as a Christian, your spirit will become diseased and grow all kinds of atrocious thoughts and may even call them godly. The Lord's desire for you is to grow healthy spiritually. Just like a child's development, spiritual growth is progressive. Each experience, each decision, each day offers an opportunity to develop. As you develop, you become more and more of a resource to others who are less developed than you and to your brothers and sisters in Christ.

"But also for this very reason, giving all diligence, add to your faith virtue, to virtue knowledge, to knowledge self-control, to self-control perseverance, to perseverance godliness, to godliness brotherly kindness, and to brotherly kindness love. For if these things are yours and abound, you will be neither barren nor unfruitful in the knowledge of our Lord Jesus Christ. For he who lacks these things is shortsighted, even to blindness, and has forgotten that he was cleansed from his old sins. Therefore, brethren, be even more diligent to make your call and election sure, for if you do these things you will never stumble; for so an entrance will be supplied to you abundantly into the everlasting kingdom of our Lord and Savior Jesus Christ," 2 Peter 1:5-11.

Stepping Stones

1. Deliverance is the act of being rescued or set free from bondage and sin.

2. Transformation begins by renewing your mind.

3. You have two enemies: you and satan.

4. You must want to be free, or you will remain bound in your sin.

5. Deliverance frees you to serve God and others fully.

6. Walking in deliverance and transformation will allow your gifts to grow and your spiritual fruit to mature.

7. Your transformation will strengthen your relationship with God, and your relationship with God will bring more transformation. It's all relative.

8. Transformation will develop Christ-like characteristics.

9. You will learn who you are and what your purpose is in your new identity as a child of God.

10. Tools for walking out your deliverance are reading the Word, praying, and spending time with other believers.

I Thought I Was Changed

WALKING IN TRANSFORMATION

1. What is deliverance?

2. What areas of my life need deliverance?

3. What Christ-like characteristics do I need to work on developing?

4. What steps can I take toward transformation to be more like Christ?

5. Self-evaluation: What hindrances limit my growth?

6. What victories have I experienced in my life?

VICTORY IN CHRIST SCRIPTURES

Deuteronomy 20:4

Psalm 44:6-8

2 Corinthians 2:14

1 Corinthians 15:57

1 John 2:12-15

1 John 3:8

James 1:12-15

1 John 5:3-5

Revelation 3:21

1 John 4:4

Revelation 12:11

Glossary

Adultery - The act of being sexually unfaithful to one's spouse

Agape - Affection, goodwill, love, brotherly love, a love feast

Angel - Messenger of God

Apostasy - Turning away from the religion, faith, or principles that one used to believe

Apostle - One sent forth, one chosen and sent with a special commission as a fully authorized representative of the sender.

Atonement - To cover, blot out, forgive; restore harmony between two individuals.

Attribute – An inherent characteristic

Backslide - To go back to ungodly ways of believing or acting.

Blasphemy - Words or actions showing a lack of respect for God or anything sacred.

Bless - To make or call holy, to ask God's favor, to praise; to make happy.

Blessing - A prayer asking God's favor for something, something that brings joy or comfort.

Born-again – To be begotten or birthed from God, the beginning, to start anew

Carnal - Of the flesh or body, not of the spirit, worldly; seat of one's desires opposed to the spirit of Christ

Cherubim - Guardian angels, angels that guard or protect places

Commitment - A promise, a pledge

Conditional - Placing restrictions, conditions, or provisions to receive

Conversion - Turn, return, turn back; change

Convert - To change from one form or use to another, to change from one belief or religion to another.

Courtship - The act or process of seeking the affection of one with the intent of seeking to win a pledge of marriage

Covenant - A pledge, alliance, agreement

Cult - A body of believers whose doctrine denies the deity of Christ.

Deliverance - A freeing or being freed, rescue; the act of change or transformation.

Demon - Evil spirit

Devil - Principal title for satan, the archenemy of God and man

Dispensation - A period of time, sometimes called ages

Dominion - To rule over, have power over, overcome, exercise lordship over

Eros - Erotic, physical love

Eternal - Existing always, forever, without time

Evangelist - Proclaims the gospel of Jesus Christ

Faith - Believing, trusting, depending, and relying on God

Fellowship - Sharing, communion, partnership, intimacy

Forgiveness - To pardon, release from bondage

Fornication - To act like a harlot, to be unfaithful to God, illicit sexual intercourse

Glorification - Salvation of the body, transforming mortal bodies to eternal bodies

Grace - Unmerited favor of God, help given in the time of need from a loving God

Holy - Set apart, sacred

Intercession - To meet or encounter, to strike upon, to pray for another

Justification - Salvation of the spirit, just as if I never sinned

Marriage - A divine institution designed by God as an intimate union, which is physical, emotional, intellectual, social, and most importantly, spiritual

New Testament - Text of the new covenant

Offering - Everything you give beyond your tithe

Old Testament - Text of the old covenant

Omnipotent - All-encompassing power of God

Omnipresent - Unlimited nature of God, ability to be everywhere at all times

Omniscient - God's power to know all things

Pastor - Shepherds of the body of believers

Philia - Conditional love, based on feelings, friendships

Praise - Thanksgiving, to say good things about, words that show approval.

Prayer - Communication with God

Prophet - One who is a spokesperson for God, one who has seen the message of God and declares that message

Propitiation - To satisfy the anger of God, to gain favor; appease

Rapture - To be carried away, or the catching away of

Reconciliation - Restore harmony or fellowship between individuals, to make friendly again

Redemption - To buy back, to purchase, recover, to Rescue from sin

Regeneration - To give new life or force to, renew, to be restored, to make better, improve or reform, to grow back anew

Repent - To give new life or force, to renew, to be restored, to make better, improve or reform, to grow back a new.

Resurrection - A return to life subsequent to death

Revelation - The act of revealing or making known

Righteousness - Right standing with God, integrity, virtue, purity of life, correctness of thinking

Sacrifice - The act of offering something, giving one thing for the sake of another; a loss of profit

Salvation - Deliverance from any kind of evil whether material or spiritual, being saved from danger or evil; to rescue.

Sanctification - Salvation of the soul. Separation from the seduction of sin

Satan - The chief of fallen spirits, opponent; adversary

Sealing - Something that guarantees, a sign or token, to make with a seal to make it official or genuine

Sin - All unrighteousness, missing the mark, wrong or fault; violation of the law

Spirit - A being that is not of this world, has no flesh or bones

Steward - A guardian or overseer of someone else's property, manager

Supernatural - Departing from what is usual, normal, or natural to give the appearance of transcending the laws of nature

Talent - A natural skill that is unusual.

Tithe - Ten percent of all your increase

Tribulation - Distress, trouble, a pressing together, pressure, affliction

Trinity - Three in one: Father, Son, Holy Spirit

Unconditional - No restrictions, conditions, boundaries, demands, or specific provisions

Will – Choice, inclination, desire, pleasure, command, what one wishes or determines shall be done

About the Author

Pamela is a teacher, mentor, and author of the inspirational book *Destiny Arise* and children's books including *Time in a Tuna*. Pam earned her bachelor's degree at the University of Illinois Springfield, her master's degree in Organizational Leadership at Lincoln Christian University, and her doctorate in Leadership at Christian Leadership University. She serves as a mentor for the Spirit Life Circles sponsored by CLU.

She works from her home in the prairie land of central Illinois. Pam and her bodybuilding husband own a gym/fitness center that promotes living a balanced life. She taught sixth grade for almost twenty years. Pam also taught preschool through adult-age students in various venues. She served as director of Super Church, the children's ministry in the United Methodist Church in her hometown. Pam also served in the church nursery, as director of New Life Ministries Discipleship Program, Vacation Bible School Director, Kingdom Kids Children's Ministry Director, and Sunday School teacher. She has also been on missionary trips. Her favorite trip, so far, was the time she spent in Belize.

Pam enjoys kayaking, bicycling, and riding her motor scooter. When she isn't writing, she enjoys spending time with her four children and their families which includes five grandchildren who are the inspiration of her children's books.

Walking with Jesus Series

BECOMING THE BEST ME I CAN BE

Book 1 - There Must Be a Better Way

Walking in Salvation

Book 2 - Lord, I Need Help!

Walking with the Holy Spirit

Book 3 - I Thought I Was Changed

Walking in Transformation

Book 4 - I Am Supernatural

Walking in Spiritual Gifts

Book 5 - I Am Strong

Walking as a Warrior

Book 6 - I Am Fruitful

Walking in the Fruit of the Spirit

Book 7 - Love Letters from God

Walking in the Word

Book 8 - Time in the Garden

Walking in the Power of Prayer

Book 9 - I'm in Charge of What?

Walking in Stewardship

Book 10 - The End of – Well, Pretty Much Everything

Walking into Eternity

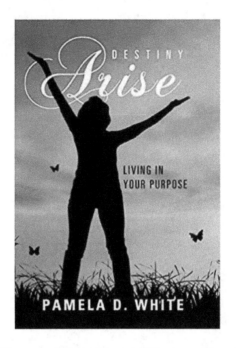

Who am I? What am I doing here? Where am I going? Everyone at some point in life asks these questions. You were wired to ask and engineered to pursue the answers. The road to discovering destiny is besieged by fiascoes, failures, and the agony of defeat. If your strength has been depleted and has caused you to give up, sit down, push pause, and snooze until another day, then this book is just for you! Amazing experiences are waiting for you. Get ready to be awakened from the posture of defeat, depression, and despair.

Destiny Arise is an easy-to-read book, providing tools to aid in living an amazing life. This book is designed as a trip adviser for your expedition. It will teach you how to evict the spirit of mediocrity and use your past to propel you into your future. You will learn how to shake off the common, arising to be an uncommon force taking your rightful place in the earth. You can change the world. I pray this book will ignite a passionate fire to pursue your destiny unapologetically. Destiny, awake from your slumber and arise.